The Journey of Self-Care

from the Inside Out

Empowering Leaders and Emerging Leaders

for Today and Tomorrow

JAMES M. BAKER, Jr.

TRUE PERSPECTIVE PUBLISHING HOUSE

The Journey of Self-Care from the Inside Out:
Empowering Leaders and Emerging Leaders for Today and Tomorrow

Printed in the United States of America

ISBN 978-1-7340305-0-1

Cover Design by Eboni Hogan

Dedication

May this book commemorate each who touched my life in a profound manner; who have transitioned, and those who are living and leading now. I honor each of you in love:

In Memory of:

My Parents

James M. Baker, Sr.

Ambassador Shirley Baker

GREAT GRANDMOTHER

Janet Knowles

Grandparents

Dr. W.O. and Inez Girtman

Leroy and Orene Baker

Aunts

Evangelist Vivian Kelly

Mary Ramsay

1st Lady Evelyn Girtman

Allie Girtman

Uncles

Charles Baker

David Lee

Brooks Baldwin

James Girtman

Bishop Aaron Kelly, Sr.

Cousins

Dara Lee

Bert Baker

Pete Baker

Chuck Baker

Roland Omega

Thurston Gross

Friends

Terry Cleckley

Keith Alexander

Mrs. Elcock

Regina Elcock

Nathaniel White

Derrick Godbold

Mrs. Elsie Banks

Mr. Willie Davis

Mrs. Keither Smith

Elder James Proctor Sr.

Scott VanPutten

Carlos Rojas Sr.

Kenny Shaw

God Parents

Mr. and Mrs. Ezekiel Pankey

Living and Leading in the 21st Century

My Uncle - Apostle Robert Girtman

My Aunt - Bishop Michel White Haynes

My Aunt -Bishop Marva Baldwin

Deacon William Girtman II

Special Recognition

My Aunt Mary Lee

My Aunt Shirley Wilson

Sylvia my personal Encourager

My Roots

Honorable Acknowledgements

I served in Ministry at the Church of the living God, where the late Dr. W. O. Girtman and Dr. I. E. Girtman were the founders and are my beloved grandparents. I come from a family of leaders and preachers within the Church of the living God. However, I transitioned to start Grace and Truth Ministries in 2013 until 2017; and in 2018 shifted to what is now known as Grace and Truth Leadership organization. I served as the Pastor and worked primarily out of my home, and these were some of the most enriching years of my life.

I am a son, husband, father, grandfather, brother, nephew, uncle, cousin, and friend to those God has placed in my life. Building many relationships over the years has changed the trajectory of my life for the better, forever. My beloved parents, the late James Baker Sr. and Mother Ambassador Shirley Baker are without question my most significant influences along with my big sister, who is also like my mom, Angela Baker Harrison and are where I established my foundation.

I learned how to be a servant leader watching them in life embrace the assignment of serving others in non-traditional ways. My wife, Robin

Baker, has supported me through this fantastic journey, her contributions are significant to any success realized and experienced, and I am grateful and love her to life. My beloved daughter, Ashley Baker, is integral to my leadership team, and I love her with all my heart.

My Fruits

Special Acknowledgements

To my family, each of you has touched my life and has made an impact beyond words, and I love each of you especially all my daughters Eboni, Nia, Imani, Aunts, Uncles, and cousins. I honor my special relationships with my beloved grandchildren, Amiyah, Avery, DJ, and Tristan some of my greatest blessings to my life. My brother-in-law Bobby, my niece Jennifer love you and husband Melvin and children Meliya, Mariah and our baby Heaven. Covenant family Leader Elder Aaron (cousin and brother) Accountability partner more now than ever, Leader Pastor Gene (cousin and brother) inspiration more now than ever, and Protector William (cousin and brother), musician Steven (cousin and brother) quiet strength.

Board of directors for my life, one of my Spiritual advisors Dr. Linwood Bush your love, leadership, and regard towards me has given me life and has become a father in my life. Senior Corporate Executive Craig Ivey, one of the greatest leaders to influence my life in its entirety, and your belief in me has transformed my life. CEO, Teressa Moore-Griffin an amazing leadership coach of all coaches to touch my life professionally and personally words can't express. Senior Wealth advisor Anthony Shropshire is amazing in financial empowerment and my little brother; you are a gift to my life. CEO, Beth Clark is an incredible diversity inclusion consultant and one of my personal coaches that have impacted my life tremendously. Last but not least, my subject matter expert in my presentations, Michelle, thank you.

To all those that I have the privilege to coach and mentor, you all are a treasure to my life from the Lord.

To my Red Hook Brooklyn family, my building 38 Bush Street and to all of you in all of the other buildings and blocks please know you hold a place for life in my heart.

To all my colleagues in ministry and the corporate world, you've touched my life deeply. My union, Brother and understudy Daleel, you stuck with me. To my leadership and prayer conference call family, the marketplace prayer and bible study family, where would I be without each of you. Lastly, to every leader and pastor who took a chance on my giftings in allowing me to share with you and your congregation for the last 20 years, I thank and honor you.

Why I Wrote This Book

The journey of self-care from the inside out is vital to my leadership sustainability. It's a subject matter that is relevant to leaders and emerging leaders for today and tomorrow. My leadership experience is the composition of 38 years of working in Corporate America and 20 years of Ministry all in the role of servant leadership. Be advised that the leadership principles and guidance in the content of this book are fully interchangeable for your professional careers and personal circumstances. Self-Care from the inside out remains intricately connected to one's ability to love, lead, and live the abundant life, (John 10:10 NKJV). Self-Care is predicated on the fundamental leadership basics if you are not able to lead yourself, you will not be able to lead anyone else.

Author and motivational speaker John Maxwell contends that "everything rises and falls with leadership." Leadership is integral to the success or demise of any organization. I'm contending in this journey that people, families, businesses, and churches are at their core constructed organizationally. Self-Care creates value for self and others. In its highest purpose, potential and possibilities, self-care can build the most exceptional people, families, businesses, and churches this world has ever realized.

Jesus practiced Self-Care in the Garden of Gethsemane. I reflected explicitly on one of Jesus' most challenging times in the Garden of Gethsemane the night before he was crucified and died. It struck me that He must have been feeling weighed down by some very acute emotions that all of us experience at various times in our lives: fear, loneliness, and a sense of failure. I've discovered all successful leaders experience painful times, but if they can endure, they create value for themselves and the lives they will ultimately touch.

Incredibly powerful were those feelings that, as the Gospel of Luke tells us, "his sweat became like drops of blood falling on the ground" (Luke 22:44 NKJV). This experience is not a hyperbole but a medical phenomenon: Under severe emotional stress, the small capillaries can become so infused with blood that they burst, allowing blood to leak through the sweat glands. Knowing what was ahead of him, it is understandable that Jesus would be overwhelmed by his emotions. Luke's description of this compelling scene invites us to engage in deeper reflection and consider times when we, too, have succumbed to our feelings. Self-Care from the inside out is on display in these times. Persevering and successful people know who they are, and are clear about what matters to them.

However, the realization was unmistakable: Jesus could not count on the emotional and spiritual support of even his best friends. The Master would have to face his sufferings alone (Matthew 26:39-41 NKJV). This encounter is what resonated with me upon wanting to share this self-care journey and its significance.

Self-Care makes you accountable for your personal development. I am proposing that leaders who embrace self-care in their life's journey must never stop evolving. They are lifelong learners and are always looking for ways to be the best version of themselves.

I look at the lives of some celebrity people I admire: Michael Jackson, Whitney Houston, Anthony Bourdain, Carrie Fisher, and Spiritual leaders Pastor Zachary Timms, Pastor Andrew Stoecklein, and Pastor Isaac Hunter. These celebrities and pastors had some very unique similarities. They were unable to find a way to care for themselves adequately. Having a significant impact on the lives of people through artist entertainment and spiritual leaders' inner attainment, not understanding how to care for themselves wholesomely led to their tragic demise. There is no lack of statistics about pastors, and depression, burnout, health, low pay, spirituality, relationships and longevity, and none of them are good. According to the Schaeffer Institute, "70 percent of pastors constantly fight depression, and 71 percent are burned out." We all have to contend with the self-care leadership practice in our various life journeys.

My life has been an ongoing struggle of learning how to apply effective self-care practices. I realize more than ever that it will be either my ability or inability to deploy self-care from the inside out of fulfilling my purpose in life. If I don't have my emotional health as a priority in my life, I am a casualty waiting to happen. Please hear my heart. It's not my gifts, talents, and abilities that are the priority, but my emotional health is more important than anything else. My gifts, talents, and skills are what I give out to others. My emotional health is who I am inside the person of James Baker Jr.

My mission with this book is to empower your life, your emotional intelligence, and self-awareness capabilities to the fullest extent. It is to equip you with knowledge and tools as you serve your children as parent leaders, serve in your careers as professional leaders, serve in your churches as ministry leaders, serve in our world as community leaders, and serve each other as our sisters' and brothers' keeper. We must have a mindset that understands there is a time to give out, and there is a time to go inside to be restored, replenished, and reignited to complete the journey of living your greatest life now. I am overwhelmingly grateful for this being my first book, to have tapped into my potential, my purpose, and what God's plan is for my life.

The purpose of this book is to help you focus on self-care practices for wholeness in mind, body, and spirit. I am not writing on this subject to give any credit to "self" for "selfie" reasons. The word "self" today connects to a "selfie" generation. Selfie pictures and selfie sticks create a thought-process of self-absorption. Being self-centered is essentially not fulfilling and leaves people feeling empty.

Conversely, focusing on serving other people, cultivates higher purpose and fulfillment. Helping others offsets the selfish and self-centered proclivities of our human nature. My contention is in the pouring ourselves out for the sake of others. We need to have the means to receive, recalibrate, and be restored. My self-care approach intends to alter these understandings to an "altar-ed" space of first caring for the self.

Moreover, before you can fully love and be in relationship with others, you must first love you. I liken this to travel on an airplane. Before departure, the airline attendants include this one rule during their oxygen instructions announcements. In the event of a decompression, an oxygen mask will automatically appear in front of you. To start the flow of oxygen, first pull the mask towards yourself. Place it firmly over your nose and mouth, secure the elastic band behind your head, and breathe normally. At this point, after you have secured first your wellbeing, you are then in a position to help anyone who needs assistance. Another noteworthy person tells you to love yourself as well as our neighbors (Mark 12:30-31 NIV). I am submitting for your consideration that the heart of self-care is a matter of life and death figuratively and literally. I have been on a mission to empower, encourage, and engage in the transformational leadership work currently as a servant leader: Coaching, Consulting, Counseling, and Praying with all I have in me.

Foreword

Craig S. Ivey, Senior Executive Leader, Corporate America

Self-care is a concept that is likely a blind spot for most good leaders. Good leaders think and act in an outward fashion. Communicating and aligning the organization and its people around vision, strategy, and execution while delivering positive results is the focus of leaders. This work requires extraordinary energy, persistence, and patience. This work is difficult. Imagine the goal of convincing hundreds of people to adopt, as their own, a most singular point of view about the direction of the organization.

When James described the concept of self-care to me, it made perfect sense. At that moment, I realized two things: I had a blind spot, and James knew it. He had spent many hours over the course of several years fulfilling a need that I didn't know I had. In retrospect, I realize the value of those regular interactions. James was helping to restore the energy and spirit that I needed to continue to lead and give the required support to the organization.

A way for leaders to think about the concept of self-care is analogous to banking. A bank account receives deposits which are credits and withdrawals which are debits. It's important for the account to be balanced daily to avoid serious issues. Leaders need balance too. The daily grind of leading produces debits. Good leaders are able to restore through quiet reflection and recalibration. Over time debits accumulate and can produce deficits that can be too large to be overcome with daily reflection.

Strong leaders are unlikely to correctly diagnose this growing deficit. Leaders provide support and don't think about the need for self-care. This is why a coach, mentor, or advisor is so critically important to leaders. We need someone that can identify those blind spots and help us restore balance in our lives. James did that for me, and I'm eternally grateful.

Craig Ivey is a prominent corporate leader within the nation's utility industry. His long and distinguished leadership career earned him positions as a member of the Board of Directors, President, and as Senior Vice President at several leading utility companies across America.

Table of Contents

Chapter 1

Self-Care: Not as You Know or Like

I begin with a question: In what ways does self-care benefit and impact our minds, bodies, and spirits? If you're anything like most leaders, then you know that we rarely take care of the more valuable assets that God wants us to maintain daily. We are in charge of our minds, bodies, and spirits. God trusts you to do the right thing with these three areas of your life. He desires above all "that we prosper and be in good health even as our souls prosper" (3 John 2 NKJV).

However, we lack knowledge on this subject. Self-care, for the most part, is not taught in the home at child-rearing. Neither is it taught in our seminaries, our college institutions, or in our local churches. It's something we learn later in life, primarily through negative experiences—

if at all. We are mainly taught and instructed to "give of self" and to provide a service, rarely if at all taught about self-care.

Consequently, some leaders don't pay attention to their bodies and what it speaks daily. Your body will talk to you. This earthly tabernacle will tell you when to rest, proper nourishment and water are needed. The body also has a way of responding to how you treat it. For example, I recently read a testimony from a leader-pastor who stayed in the hospital for five days due to severe stomach issues. Here's the lead-pastors account:

About a week ago, a visit to the ER for what I thought was agonizing stomach pain, turned into a 5-day hospital stay for an intestinal infection, inflammation, fatigue, and stress. I had the symptoms for about two weeks and took over the counter meds, and continued to do my regular routines. I pushed my body too far, and it showed. I wasn't eating correctly, or resting correctly, and it caught up with me. I honestly didn't know the state of my body until the hospital stay. Often, we blame the devil in situations like this. I can't give him that credit. I take responsibility for what I did to my physical body. I can't get to my next in the kingdom if

I don't take care of my body. The doctors treated me and gave me a plan of action to get on the road of recovery. I will do my part to eat right, avoid unnecessary stresses, and get proper rest weekly.

Please don't ignore your body signals. People, especially preachers and leaders, please take note that self-care is the best care. We can't preach health and wealth and don't first be examples.

As spiritual leaders, we must seek inner growth of character, wisdom, and obedience more than outer growth of ministry impact. Yes, we want both, but we need to observe that we are in the Word of God, reading good books, spending time around mentors, as well as watching the overall health of our soul, relationships and emotions more than we are giving out. This can be tricky for Pastors who are preaching every week. Sundays come with surprising regularity. However, simple ways to work toward this end would be:

- Set time for healthy growth habits once a week

- Plan growth time in your schedule just like you plan out your to-do list

- Schedule another pastor to preach once or twice a month in your place to give you more time for intake than giving out.

Author and motivational speaker Jim Rohn contends that "self-care is not selfish. Nor is it a waste of time. Self-care isn't about perfection or tricking yourself. It's an honest internal dialog, which is where the challenge lies. Most of us aren't accustomed to giving a truthful answer to the 'how are you' question at the "water cooler." How many respond to this question honestly. The pastor above probably continued her routines in ministry and life, thinking she was fine until her body said otherwise. Self-care most certainly benefits our minds, bodies, and spirits. This daily practice contributes to your wholeness and effectiveness. As you take this journey of self-care, you will be answering many questions about yourself, your passions, your giftings, your goals, and more. However, in a greater sense, all those questions will make known your life's purpose, your potential, and the possibilities of your destiny.

Self-Care leaders can step into their optimal sense of purpose, potential, and possibilities for their life because they have a self-awareness that gives them a decisive edge. Understanding self-care is a life or death matter for all of us, identifying what we need to learn, relearn, and unlearn; the trajectory of our life depends on it. Author and Christian apologist C.S. Lewis said it best, "You are never too old to set another goal or dream a new dream." Understanding self-care principles is the key that unlocks the door to your life of :

- personal development

- professional development

- problem-solving

These developmental components are significant so that you can live life in the best version of yourself now.

Chapter 2

Leadership & Self-care

Leadership has been one of my greatest pursuits in life. I have not always operated in this responsibility like a husband, father, family member, co-worker, and ministry leader as I would have liked. However, I have learned some valuable lessons about leadership that will add significant value to any leader. I have invested more than nineteen years of my life in helping myself and others about leading.

I've learned through my leadership development, which is still emerging and will be until the end of my days. One of the highest components of leadership begins with yourself. Once you have invested in yourself purposefully, you can start to invest in others. As a leader, you don't coach people to go where you have not gone. You need to call people to where you are. Dr. Martin Luther King Jr., powerfully shared, "Life's most persistent and urgent question is, what are you doing for others?"

Our effectiveness as leaders of any type remains intricately connected to demonstrating what we want our people to do and then sharing our successes and failures with them. We go together, or we go nowhere at all, and I believe this with all my heart. It would be best if you met people where they are and discover the next steps together. This also means that people need to have their own invested interest. When they are a part of the solution, they become part of the outcome.

I am hopeful and yet have a great concern about the future of leadership as we have experienced it traditionally. I've asked dozens of leaders consisting of pastors, managers, supervisors, fathers, mothers, community advocates, teachers, and entrepreneurs, to describe their self-care practices. Their answers vary due to the category and, their leadership role and function.

It is my premise that self-care is particularly crucial for whatever role of leadership you serve in, remember to establish effective self-care practices that empower you as a leader. I am urging leaders of all types to practice self-care discipline, and that way, you can develop healthy boundaries and create a sense of balance, even in the face of a challenging life and interpersonal environments. Taking care of yourself is not selfish; it's effective.

Making time to recharge and tap into your sources of inspiration are imperative when your life and concerns are not only demanding but also demands that you be there for others. We must be mindful of the tendency of self-sabotage when self-care is not a daily practice in our lives. Leaders and emerging leaders can take proactive measures to ensure they are practicing self-care in and outside of the interpersonal environments they co-exist. Getting enough rest, so we can function in our lives rested, praying, or meditating so we feel centered, relaxed, and balanced and ready to inspire others, we interface with, in a productive, effective manner. However, it is also essential to consider self-care as the optimal response to moments where we have made mistakes.

In other words, self-punishment should not be a convenient alternative to self-care in the face of mistakes we've made. Kristin Neff, Ph.D. and Associate Professor at the University of Texas at Austin, has written extensively on the importance of a concept she calls "self-compassion." Neff identifies the difference between self-esteem and self-compassion — noting that "self-compassion does not rely on external circumstances but is always available because each human can and deserves to be understood." So part of self-care involves the art of accepting every part of who we are. Moreover, if that includes a mistake in a given moment, that is okay. Often, we are tested not to discover our weaknesses but to discover our strengths.

The story of Samson one of Israel's judges resonates with me from a self-care perspective. There's a Samson in every man and woman if we are not able to practice self-care. Not because every man is destined to lose his power, but because every man or woman is vulnerable without a strong sense of soul care and spiritual connection as the source of our sustainability. Samson was gifted with supernatural strength, and was developed by God for leadership; he had two unique blessings:

- a divine calling on his life

- two Godly parents who offered him love and guidance.

However, it becomes apparent that Samson didn't know or understand how to care for himself in a wholesome manner. In the life of Samson, we get a glimpse that leadership can be a lonely and isolated and insulated life. Samson chooses the wrong person and place to be restored and replenished. He placed his head in the lap of Delilah, and money and his demise motivated her. Samson was obsessed by his desire for personal pleasure, and it cost his life (Judges 16:16-30 NIV). The absence of self-care does weaken our moral and spiritual strength, and we very likely can be susceptible to the influence of self- sabotage. Samson thought what he needed was outside of himself, but the care he needed was within himself; it's called self-care.

Chapter 3

Called to Live a Self-care Fulfilled Life

Your calling in life is not the same as your neighbor's. However, God calls you to take care of yourself. Is it a sacrifice? Absolutely! Can you master this part of the call from God? Indeed! The question is: will you answer the call? This part of living requires sacrifice and a life of dedication and being set apart per se.

Many scripture references reveal the call for self-care and what to do with our bodies. Here are a few for your consideration:

: I Corinthians 6:19-20 NIV
19 Do you not know that your bodies are temples of the Holy Spirit, who is in you, whom you have received from God? You are not your own; 20 you were bought at a price. Therefore, honor God with your bodies.

I Corinthians 3:16-17 NIV

16 Don't you know that you yourselves are God's temple and that God's Spirit dwells in your midst? 17 If anyone destroys God's temple, God will destroy that person; for God's temple is sacred, and you together are that temple.

Romans 12: 1 NIV

1 Therefore, I urge you, brothers and sisters, in view of God's mercy, to offer your bodies as a living sacrifice, holy and pleasing to God—this is your true and proper worship.

The Apostle Paul gently reminds us of our call and duty to practice self-care for our bodies. If you're part of the same background as me, these scriptures are often repeated to us using different contexts. Rarely are they used or viewed as a call to and duty for self-care. Moreover, the whole meaning of these words and more not mentioned here is taking care of you. Self-care is a vocation for everyone. Self-care is our duty, and it pleases God. Think about how God, after creation for six days, rested on day seven (Genesis 2:2 NKJV). God has not only provided an example for self-care. The Lord has also sent out a call to the universe to follow and expand our self-care regimens.

Once you answer the "self-care call" and start to make it apart of your life, there are many rewards you'll reap. Plus, you enter into a fulfilled place in life. I often tell my clients and church members this dimension of living brings you into vibrant living. God desires nothing less than for you and me to experience all life has to offer (John 10:10 NKJV).

However, when your body gets attacked from eating the wrong foods and over-stressed from continually going here and there, you'll find it difficult to hear this call for your life completely. These vices block you from the sound of God's call. I know for sure that self-care is of great consequence for ministry leaders (Ephesians 4:1 NKJV), and leaders of all vocations to walk worthy of which is pleasing to God (Colossians 1:10 NKJV).

This is all tied to knowing your value. How do you feel about yourself? When you know who you are, then you will discover who you are in God. God calls us the pearl of high value (Matthew 13:46 ESV). This passage is simply saying we are God's creation, and the Master of the universe greatly values us. Pearls originate from the oyster. The oyster appears to be just another barnacle-covered shell of little value, and like this pearl, we cannot tell someone's worth by looking at them. However, the Lord can see within. He can look into our hearts and see the quality that lies within each of us.

The longer the pearl stays in the oyster, the more valuable it gets. When we started, we were nothing more than an irritation, but the longer we spend applying the covering of Christ to ourselves, the more precious we become, and by God's grace we can be of some value to His kingdom. Practicing self-care is a strong indication of how you value yourself.

Chapter 4

How Change Prepares You for Self-care

IF A MAN DIES, SHALL HE LIVE AGAIN? ALL THE DAYS OF MY HARD SERVICE I WILL WAIT, TILL MY CHANGE COMES. (JOB 14:14 NKJV).

The one constant thing in your life is the need for change. You cannot avoid change, and the more you resist change, the tougher your life becomes. Change can come into your life from a crisis, a choice, or by the call of destiny. In either situation, you have to decide whether to make the change or not. It is always better to make proactive changes in your life when making choices rather than being reactive. However, many times, the needed change for your life and destiny is through a crisis. Do you know you are the change that's necessary for your life?

For some of us, it takes a crisis to admit a need for help. We may experience an emergency where we come close to death. In other instances, we may feel overwhelmed by depression, suicidal thoughts, and self-destructive behaviors. Sometimes it is our hopelessness and crisis that acts as a catalyst, shifting us to change the direction of our lives. When we realize that we are at the end of ourselves, we may find the humility to reach out and accept the help and change we need. Change is something we face at several junctures in our lives. Always keep in mind, "Strength doesn't come from what you can do. It comes from overcoming the things you once thought you couldn't" urges Writer and marketer, Rikki Rogers.

Our ability to embrace change for our lives will determine our destiny. We, however, cannot avoid the unexpected life crisis in our lives because it is these events that challenge our complacency in life. What we can control when we are experiencing these challenging life crises, is how we choose to respond to them. It is our power of decision-making that enables us to activate positive change in our lives. Acting on our power of choice provides us with more opportunities to change our lives for the better. The more opportunities we create to change our lives, the more fulfilled and wholesome our lives become.

When we have reached our darkest hour and feel that all hope is lost, we may be closer to the help we need for our life's purpose. When crisis of pain, death, loss, health, and finances stares us in the face, and we realize that our cup is empty, we can lift our empty cup by admitting our powerlessness, and thus, open up to the Lord's salvation for our lives as King David declares (Psalm 116:12 KJV). The leadership of Job is an excellent example of change. Job embraced that the shift he needed was in himself and trust in the Lord. The profound words of world-renowned Mother Teresa seem to be the sentiment of Job's leadership message, "I know God will not give me anything I can't handle. I just wish He didn't trust me so much."

Consider these suggestions to work towards change in your life for self-care from a crisis.

Please spend some time trying to sort out what is essential in your life and why it is crucial.

What is it that you want to achieve in your life? What are your dreams? What makes you fulfilled?

- Remember you are the change you need for your own life

- Create a Board Directors for your life

- Make peace with your past

- Develop your personal Prayer life

- Begin reading more personal development Books

- Remember to make sure your plans align with God's plan for your life (Jeremiah 29:11 NKJV).

Chapter 5

The Grass is Greener

O ne day while scrolling my feed on Instagram, I came across the heart of my message about self-care by Bishop T.D. Jakes. He perfectly captured what leaders do, how we perform our daily and monthly tasks and offered a poignant perspective about leadership and self-care.

Self-care is essential. Allowing your mind to just go into chill mode is renewing. It may take me a while, but I'm going to overcome this proclivity to give every waking moment of my life to responding to other's needs or working on the next deal at the inflated expense of denying myself normalcy and renewable tranquility. Simply put, I'm going to try to be better for me! ~T.D. Jakes 2019

Leaders have the mentality that busy means success, and the grass is greener on the other side. I am guilty of this, too. For three decades, I spent more time preparing for sermons, seminars, and bible studies. I work hard at being a problem solver for other people's issues, making sure I'm a supporter to my friends and family, meeting the needs of those in the pews, traveling, writing, and was diligent at my nine to five up to retirement. I also lead a live weekly prayer call with a significant number of attendees. I consult and coach other leaders in the areas of transformation, finance, community involvement, and tending to the elderly. After my retirement, God began to speak to my heart about self-care.

During this moment, the best revelation came to my spirit. The grass is not greener because of money, riches, or accomplishments. It's greener because of self-care and living a vibrant life and abundant life. Sadly, the millennial leaders I coach and consult with do not know this side to life and living. Those that I speak with are more in love with great opportunities, which adds lots of wear and tear on their bodies and creates mental exhaustion. Of course, when you're young, the emotions of excitement sparks that adrenaline from the new doors that open. Who doesn't want greatness, money, more speaking engagements, and a household name? Moreover, please understand my point; these things are incredible. I'm merely telling you that the grass is truly greener when you include the right tools for self-care.

Have you ever driven in an upscale neighborhood and noticed the healthy, green grass? The grass is fertile, vital, and rich in color. These homeowners take care of their lawns with proper fertilizers, seeds, and water. Nature adds the necessary sunshine and rain. Your body and mind are no different. After the large doors for opportunity open, both of them need proper nourishment and care. Many leaders wither away because of a lack of self-care. It's not a good thing or practice to look exceptional on the outside and have a void on the inside. Even the scripture warns us about keeping the outside clean and ignoring the inside. (Matthew 15:16-20 NIV)

My heart has a massive place for Millennials and the Gen Z generation because they matter, and I care deeply for them. Having children and grandchildren from each of these generations is sobering and compelling for me. I believe sincerely that every generation has the responsibility of passing the baton to the next generation. Succession planning is a vital part of finishing well in life. Legacy is not so much about leaving something for someone, but more about leaving something in someone. It's amazing when we realize that our success in life predicates on our ability or inability to shape our future, and take responsibility for our experience. Self-care leadership is an excellent resource for changing our lives within us, and the results show up on the outside of us.

The emphasis of the self-care leader is in developing and utilizing four vital human gifts:

- Self-awareness
- Principles
- Inspiration
- The power of making decisions

And by taking an inside-out approach to creating change. They resolve to be the creative force of change in their lives, and this is one of the most prodigious decision a person ever makes.

Chapter 6

Understanding Leadership & Self-care

So, they answered Joshua, saying, All that you command us we will do, and wherever you send us we will go. 17 Just as we heeded Moses in all things, so we will heed you. Only the Lord, your God, be with you, as He was with Moses. (Joshua 1:16 - 17 NKJV)

The influence of leadership is exponential, and we must pray for them, whether they are our choice or not. The impact of leadership on the lives of people can be useful and sometimes harmful. It has been my recent observation in the circles I travel to remain vigilant and filled with Godly values. Even if at times, I may not measure up to the challenge; one thing that is for sure it's God who authorizes leadership of any kind; we should even include President Trump in our prayers. I must confess not being a Trump supporter, but I am a leader and understand the value of prayer. There is a measure of grace given by the Lord for those in his or her assignment of leadership. I have discovered that praying for people who you may not agree with, or even someone who is in sincere need of prayer, is still helpful and it demonstrates compassion for others and could aid in creating positive change in your self-care regimen." (I Timothy 2:1-2 ESV).

We must learn the gift of encouraging the leaders in our lives now. Joshua was well trained by Moses when he took over leadership of the nation of Israel, but that was no guarantee of success. Joshua failed when he acted without first seeking God's counsel (Read Joshua Chapter 1). To encourage him, the leaders of the tribes prayed for him, saying, "Only may the Lord your God be with you as he was with Moses." When was the last time you encouraged your leader? Alternatively, are you one who encourages other leaders rather than your own?

Be mindful that being in leadership does not guarantee successful outcomes. The preeminent thing to do is to pray for our leaders. This includes leaders at every level of our society, including our families. No child of God can succeed at God's work apart from prayer. It is one of those great virtues of the people of God. Even our leaders of families, churches, and the workplace can make mistakes, but our prayers will sustain them in the grace of God! Be advised that leadership is only as influential as the impact it has on those who follow, align, and are inspired. Former first lady, Rosalyn Carter made a poignant point about leadership by saying, "A leader takes people where they want to go. A great leader takes people where they don't necessarily want to go but ought to be."

Chapter 7

Leading While Bleeding

L eadership requires many sacrifices. The numerous challenges encountered in both the physical and spiritual realm by leaders often leave them with scars and bruises that require a great deal of self-care. Combine the healing process with the task of leadership in equal measure, and do not neglect the flock as the shepherd tends to his wounds. This often means that the leader must learn to lead while bleeding and make the sacrifices required to ensure that his/her duties do not suffer as a result of their injuries.

In the bible, examples abound of leaders who were able to carry on despite being in stressful situations. Of these examples, the resilience, passion, and discipline displayed in the letters written by the apostle Paul in the books of Ephesians, Philippians, Philemon, and Colossians epitomize the virtues required to lead amid adversity or great difficulty. Despite being in prison away from the church and the other Christians, his words showed that he was able to maintain his spirit as a soldier of Christ through meticulous spiritual, mental, and emotional self-care. Also, he wrote letters to admonish and encourage other Christians who saw him as a leader and looked up to him for direction and inspiration.

This example not only emphasizes the strength of character that a Christian and all leaders need to continue leading when wounded, but it also reveals that prayer and meditation on the word of God play active roles in refreshing leaders spiritually at all times. A leader who pays attention to their inner being will be able to recover gradually and fulfill his/her responsibilities to those who follow them. Neglecting the wound and attempting to carry on without stopping the bleeding can lead to eventual death or collapse, which could spell disaster for both the leader and those who follow. It is in these situations that self-care becomes more important than ever.

Christ Jesus showed his leadership qualities in extremely precarious situations during his last days on earth. His sharp reprimand of Peter when he tried to fight back as Jesus was taken prisoner and his compassionate act of mending the injured ear of the Roman soldier, Malchus, right in the presence of His disciples is one of the most remarkable examples of sacrificial leadership (John 18:10-11 ESV). By serving as an example to his followers and practicing the same things he had been teaching in temples and open fields, Jesus showed that it is possible to lead your flock even at the point of death. It is important to note that Jesus never wavered in prayer during this period. The Lord was tending to his wounds in the best way possible by talking to God. Perhaps Jesus left on record for Peter and for all us in leadership to be careful not to become what hurt you because that's how cycles repeat themselves. I've discovered this in my life's journey as former British Prime Minister Margaret Thatcher left on record, "You may have to fight a battle more than once to win." Self-Care wins wars emotionally, psychologically, socially, economically, and relationally.

Battles are part of the life cycle of any Christian and leaders bear the brunt of these inevitable conflicts between light and darkness. Apart from this, a leader could have personal challenges like any other human being. I've discovered that people of success and God go through low moments and dark times, so we don't always have to be ok. There is no healing if you don't need help. The most important thing is to realize the need for self-care help and support to recover and be able to lead the flock in the best way possible. You can lead and bleed and win the war with self-care in your leadership repository.

Chapter 8

Ministry of Self-Care

One of the qualities of a great leader is the knack always to be perfect and also make everything or everyone around them work like a perfectly oiled machine. Sometimes the leader tends to focus on their task and forget about other important things they should focus on; particularly themselves. A leader needs to take care of what he or she has been designated to take care of, and at the same time, take care of oneself.

That's the only way you can stay healthy enough to continue your life as a leader. A sound body and mind only ensure you'll be better equipped to lead. That's why a leader needs to take self-care as a necessary precaution.

Self-care is the practice of taking a very active role in protecting your mental and physical well-being, happiness, and health. Most leaders, when asked are they taking care of themselves will answer yes, even if that's not the case. However, the real question that might be hard to answer is when asked in what way do you take care of yourself. It is important for leaders to be surrounded by caring people who can identify when their leader has taken on too much.

We get a glimpse of King David, who wanted whoever supported him to possess certain character traits. One thing David required of what is known as his "mighty men" (his leadership team) was that they work with him in peace" (V.17). King David surrounded himself as best possible with people who sought to help him not hurt him. *"¹⁶Other Benjamites and some men from Judah also came to David in his stronghold. ¹⁷ David went out to meet them and said to them, "If you have come to me in peace to help me, I am ready for you to join me. But if you have come to betray me to my enemies when my hands are free from violence, may the God of our ancestors see it and judge you."* (I Chronicles 12-16-17 NIV).

In this passage, we see King David not only sought men who worked in peace, but he also wanted to know if they had come to help him. David needed people who would be participators, not spectators of the work needed in leading people. People who are there to help often do not always acquiesce to their leaders' every desire. But these choice people that are there to help are people of unity, character, and genuine motives. These people also help leaders in their blind spots and create what I'd like to call the divine connection needed for leadership success.

Hard work is good. Self-care is also great. We all know "all work and no play makes Johnny a dull boy." The Bible says in 3 John 1:3, "Dear friends, I pray that you may enjoy good health and that all may go well with you, even as your soul is getting along well." (NIV) Romans 12:2 also states, "And be not conformed to this world and be ye changed by the renewal of your mind, that ye may prove what is good, and acceptable, and perfect will of God." (KJV) What the Bible means here is self-care on all levels is essential. When you take care of yourself, your mind is clear and sharp enough to get the full picture of God's plan for your life.

The mind functions as a machine. Even machines sometimes are turned off to rest. That's what you must do as a leader when your brain has been turned on for too long. Moreover, self-care doesn't cost you a dime, makes you more productive, improves your relationship with people around you, and gives you an added advantage mentally.

There are two ways you can take care of yourself: inner self-care, which deals with the mind and soul, and outer self-care which deals with the body. Internal self-care includes:

- Meditation or spiritual disciplines that work with your mind

- Celebrate yourself when you achieve something remarkable

- Unplug when your mind is clogged

- Do something that nourishes your brain, which isn't work-related

- Learn something new, and this strengthens your self-esteem

- Sometimes during work, take a quick power nap and notice your inner self will always feel refreshed

Outer self-care includes:

- Eating things you love in moderation.

- Exercising daily, which is excellent for the mind and body.

- Spend time with your family and friends laughing.

- Try some retail therapy (in moderation) to boost your wardrobe and mood.

- Use that beauty product that makes you look and feel good.

All of these are excellent expressions of self-care. Make sure you don't neglect any opportunity to take care of yourself and see your productivity improve, your mental and physical well-being improves, and you'll always find yourself actively engaged in your own life. In a world where so many people are disengaged in critical life matters. You'll be an active participant in your destiny.

It may be an opportunity to look at our obstacles as character builders. I have discovered we must find a way to grow through them. We must also learn the lessons that are to be gleaned in our times of challenges and obstacles. Self-Care provides an authentic resolve that all leaders need.

Chapter 9

Self-Care & Transformation

L eaders are often expected to fulfill a broad range of physical and spiritual responsibilities as they carry out the tasks assigned to their positions. This can make leaders neglect self-care at the expense of their duties. As Christian leaders, it is essential to care for our inner self by moving closer to God through Jesus Christ. Just as the body grows weary without constant nourishment, the mind and soul can become tired, stagnant, and unproductive. In such a state, it becomes difficult to lead according to the will of God.

Jesus shows this in one of the most memorable encounters during his missionary journey on earth when he turned to his disciples and told them he had compassion for these folks who had already been with him for three full days without anything to eat. The Lord refused to send them away hungry because they could collapse or perish on their way home. Having preached the gospel to a mammoth crowd for a few days, Jesus knew that it was unhealthy to remain in one place for days without eating anything to regain any strength. While this is an example from the physical standpoint, it emphasizes the need to refresh yourself and by extension, your followers from time to time as a Christian leader (Mark 8:1-9 ESV).

In Mark 1 verse 35, Jesus isolates himself from everyone else by waking up early to pray in a solitary place, where he could be alone to commune with God and renew his mind and soul through prayer and the word of God. Such acts are vital habits for leaders both as a means of self-care and as an outlet of divine instruction, which can lead to spiritual transformation.

As a Christian, you are expected to give up old habits and follow a new divine path. Reflect this change in your actions. You're a leader seen as an example for others to follow and a representative of Christ in Christendom. This improvement is not instant but comes through constant prayer and critical self-examination by reviewing your actions and going back to God at every point in time for guidance and direction. Leaders must realize the need to ask for forgiveness of their sins and asking for the compassion of God, which is sufficient at all times.

The words of the Apostle Paul in Romans 12 verse 2 places emphasis on the renewal of the mind and discerning the will of God to determine that which is right and acceptable before him. Self-care is permanently renewing the mind to remain pure. This kind of mind can receive God's instructions and help the individual to achieve transformation. A leader must maintain a balance between service, leadership, and caring for himself. The metaphorical reason is like a stagnant river cannot flow in any direction and will continue to degenerate over time because there is no outlet to release and refresh itself. Leadership comes with many challenges, but by having the leadership flow of self-care, a leader can carry out responsibilities and continue serving God transformationally at the same time.

I always remember the life story about the metamorphosis of the caterpillar into the butterfly, "The struggle is good." Once a little boy was playing outdoors and found a fascinating caterpillar. He carefully picked it up and took it home to show his mother. He asked his mother if he could keep it, and she said "yes" if he would take good care of it.

The little boy got a large jar from his mother and put plants to eat, and a stick to climb on, in the jar. Every day he watched the caterpillar and brought it new plants to eat. One day the caterpillar climbed up the stick and started acting strangely. The boy worriedly called his mother, who came and understood that the caterpillar was creating a cocoon. The mother explained that the caterpillar was going to go through a metamorphosis and become a butterfly. The little boy was thrilled to hear about the changes his caterpillar would go through. He watched every day, waiting for the butterfly to emerge. One day it happened, a small hole appeared in the cocoon, and the butterfly started to struggle to come out.

At first, the boy was excited, but soon, he became concerned. The butterfly struggled hard to get out! It looked like it couldn't break free! It looked desperate! It looked like it was making no progress! The boy was so concerned that he decided to help. He ran to get scissors and then walked back (because he had learned not to run with scissors). He snipped the cocoon to make the hole bigger, and the butterfly quickly emerged!

As the butterfly came out, the boy was surprised. It had a swollen body and small, shriveled wings. He continued to watch the butterfly expecting that, at any moment, the wings would dry out, enlarge and expand to support the swollen body. He knew that in time, the body would shrink and the butterfly's wings would expand. However, neither happened!

The butterfly spent the rest of its life crawling around with a swollen body and shriveled wings. It never was able to fly. As the boy tried to figure out what had gone wrong, his mother took him to talk to a scientist from a local college. He learned that the butterfly was supposed to struggle. The butterfly's struggle to push its way through the tiny opening of the cocoon pushes the fluid out of its body and into its wings. Without the fight, the butterfly would never, ever fly. The boy's good intentions hurt the butterfly. As you go through school, and life, keep in mind that struggling is an integral part of any growth experience. It is the struggle that causes you to develop your ability to fly. Perhaps the butterfly is proof that you, as a leader, can go through a great deal of darkness and still become something beyond human comprehension.

As I close this chapter, I have created an acronym for" Self-Care" to add to your leadership prowess and development.

The acronym for Care:

Courage

Awareness

Responsibility

Execution

In the event, you need to learn more about this leadership concept perhaps you would like to have me do a leadership seminar for your team, or you can follow me on any of my social media outlets. In addition, you can join my leadership prayer conference call held every Tuesday evening @8: 30 pm – (605) 475-3250 access code 114847# Our mission is to empower leaders and emerging leaders for today and tomorrow!

Instagram- jamesbaker_jr

Linkedin- James Baker Jr.

Twitter- @jamesbaker_jr

Facebook Business- James Baker, Jr. Grace and Truth Leadership

Facebook Personal – James Baker

Chapter 10

How Self-Care Moves You Beyond Pain

s Pope Francis has said, "The most dangerous idol is our own selves when we want to occupy the place of God." When past injustices have caused you pain, you may hurt others or often seek to bury them in the deep recesses of your mind. I needed to share with you out of the pain of my experiences. It's not the way to handle things, however, and almost always when you bury things, it allows your pain from the past to translate into mistakes and suffering in the future. You can't occupy the space of God because healing rarely occurs. The pain may feel like too much to handle. Therefore, you unintentionally block God's plan and ability to heal those places of hurt.

Are you making mistakes today because of pain from your past? You become powerless against the strength of your inner conflict and can lose control of the very feelings you have tried to hide. I know this truth because it has, and at times today is my struggle. I thought some transparency and truth could help set all of us free to live our best life now.

Here is the power lesson here "Pay close attention now: I'm creating new heavens and a new earth" (Isaiah 65:17-19 MSG). All the earlier troubles, chaos, and pain are things of the past, to let go of now. Look ahead with joy. Anticipate what God is birthing and creating through your pain. As leaders we must learn to grow the threshold of pain we can bear. There is pressure as leader and pain that must be endured as leaders. Often it will be your inability to handle the pain of your challenges that will keep you from growing and evolving into the leader of your potential, influence, and productivity.

Moreover, the best way to get beyond our pain is to get outside of it. I discovered this in my journey through a particularly dark time in my life. I decided to serve others even though I was in great emotional pain. This had a remarkable positive effect on my emotional state. Do you understand the value of helping others?

When we refocus our attention on the needs of others when we are in painful situations, it allows the burden of our circumstances to be removed and released from us. The more you focus on your problem, the more likely you are to become depressed. Isaiah, the Prophet of the Lord, understood a principle that I call "Exchange" that is still valid today. If you find yourself depressed because of a circumstance in your life, take his advice. Begin to praise the Lord in an "Exchange" of the circumstances you see. Then you will see the spirit of heaviness begin to lift because of the garment of your praise to the Lord (Read Isaiah 61:2-3 NKJV).

Many of us spend our whole lives running from "feeling" with the mistaken belief that you cannot bear the pain. However, you have already borne the pain. "What you have not done is feel all you are beyond the pain," contends Saint Bartholomew. Always remember we learn in self-care the pain in our lives serves two purposes. First to let us know something is wrong, and secondly to move us to our next place in our destiny. It's the servant leader's path and why self-care has to be intimately a part of the journey from the inside out.

Chapter 11

Next Steps: Self-care Efficient Practices for Christian Leaders

There is no disputing about the admonishment of the Apostle Paul being a prisoner of the gospel (Ephesians 3:1) or King David sharing about being a doorkeeper in the house of God than to dwell in the tents of wickedness (Psalm 84:10 NKJV). However, this text does not suggest unconscious or unintentional negligence to necessary self-care as most Christians unknowingly practice. Instead, Christian servant leaders are the most in need of regular self-caring, taking into consideration the demand of their profession and the toll it takes on them overall.

However, how necessary is this self-care? You say, "the harvest is ripe, the laborers are few." (Luke 10:2 NKJV) I am the privileged one called by God, and I must do the work. (John 5:17 NKJV) You burn the candle at both ends and melt in the middle. Self-care does not only imply exercising or a rigorous workout session. It includes the regular concern and care we give to our bodies to enable it to function better. It's like checking the oil and water level of the car before turning on the ignition is a well-accustomed practice. Why? To prevent the car engine and other components from getting in harm's way.

Similarly, Christian leaders need to regularly practice self-care if they are to function effectively in their esteemed profession. Even the Lord Jesus recommended an excellent looking appearance during periods of fasting and consecration (Matthew 6:17 NKJV). Prophet Elijah was equally advised by God to eat satisfactorily before the commissioning for the great task during the reign of King Ahab (I Kings17:2 NKJV). I believe this was done in recognition of the demanding nature of the work ahead.

Here are the next steps for quality self-care every Christian leader needs:

- Good eating habits, you may retort, I do not starve. That is true, but the emphasis here is on what you eat. The amount and type of food you consume are of crucial importance to good self-care. From the analogy of the prophet Elijah above, the ravens fed him meat and bread, because proteins and carbohydrates are a very beneficial diet. Your daily diet should also include lots of vegetables, fruits, vitamins, and necessary compounds for a better output.

Make sure you get regular physical check-ups. Check-ups can be preventive by detecting early abnormalities. Men need to have their prostate, and women need to have mammograms examinations regularly.

• Practice good relaxation. Your body is just a bundle of depreciating bones and flesh. Self-care requires you to take some time off for proper relaxation. Go on a vacation. Unwind. Do something fun other than studying scriptures and praying hard. Your body needs some pleasure. You may say, "all things are lawful, but all are not expedient" (1Corinth6:12 KJV). True, however, very importantly, "for everything, there is a season" (Ecclesiastes 3:1 KJV) so deliberately create time for relaxation. Your body will thank you for it.

• Recreations are in order, too. You are well knowledgeable on the exploits of King David, Saul, Samson, and all the biblical warriors. They gained their prowess through constant exercising. Well, I know you are not planning to get into the ring with the Heavy Weight champion of the world Deontay Wilder, but you need to get those tired muscles flexing strong, and that excess fat burned that may result in obesity or other fat-related ailments. So, go bike riding, hiking or join a gym for benefiting self-care.

• Practice great sleeping sounds incredible right? Yes, you have been sleeping, but maybe not rightly and proportionate to the stress your profession exerts on you. Self-care requires some quality sleeping for efficient output. Now for early risers, they may have a problem because the body naturally craves more sleep in the early hours and when you always deprive yourself a minimum of 6 hours of good sleep, it is terrible. Self-care suggests early sleeping as a compensation for that though.

As shepherds of God's flock, and all leaders need to give premium importance to quality self-care as it forms the foundation of excellent health, and great health is a significant determinant for better performance. The ministry and your organizations need you to be alive, as many souls are still awaiting salvation through your ministry.

Chapter 12

The Value of a Self-Care Leader

S elf-Care from the inside out provides premium value to the sustainability and the myriad of leadership modalities. It's a prerequisite for relevant leadership, and leaders in the making will find meaningful to themselves and can lead others effectively. As noted earlier in the book, self-care is predicated on the fundamental leadership basics. If you are not able to lead yourself, you will not be able to lead anyone else. Leaders who practice the power of self-care will, without doubt, emerge to be the best version of themselves. It is because they operate in the highest purpose, potential, and possibilities of leadership. Adding incredible value to one's self and building the most fabulous people, families, businesses, and churches, this world could ever imagine.

Self-care leaders are people who know themselves intimately embracing the positive and negative aspects of themselves in a valuable outcome determination. They will make significant contributions to people's lives, in professional settings, personal settings, churches, and community organizations, whatever the situation might be. They understand how to handle pressure and challenging times with resolve. They think progressively and don't operate from emotions, and they excel in meeting challenges with solid decision-making. They have a filter to utilize in the process of leadership, and that is "To Thine own self be true."

Self-care leaders are practical and pragmatic and know how to live each day with great value and seizing opportunities that emerge along the way. Their purpose always starts with self and transcends to others, which is not selfish but a servant and selfless in its ultimate purpose and scheme. Self-care leaders make the best leaders and are not the most common in the world; however, the opportunity is waiting for all to embrace.

The birth of this self-care journey for me came as a result of not knowing how to care for myself adequately. I've learned how to take care of everyone and everything else but knew very little about how to care for myself. My life has experienced addiction, divorce, rejection, and great despair because I never learned how to take care of myself. I am not necessarily a subject matter expert even as this book is published, and as you are reading right now. However, I am a little better each day and have some good moments and bad moments as well, even now. The burden of this project consumed me until I was able to share it with the world. I was compelled to share the various aspects of this book to help others, and also to help myself step into this new season of my life embracing the self-care leadership value. The value is in you, which is Christ in you the hope of glory (Colossians 1:27 NKJV).

The journey of self-care from the inside out is an amazing process realized and to be understood. To fulfill your optimal purpose, potential, and plan of God for your life, start today. It's a real journey, and it's difficult, painful with tear shedding at times, and yet well worth it. Always remember the words of author and motivational speaker Brian Tracey "Leaders think and talk about solutions. Followers think and talk about problems." My thoughts will be with you and praying for your incredible success.

About the Author

Leadership Coach. Mentor. Teacher. Motivational Speaker.

James Baker, Jr., a Red Hook Brooklyn, New York native, is the spiritual leader and founder of Grace and Truth Leadership. He is also a prolifically well-sought-after leadership coach, who helps many leaders with their call into purpose and the abundant life. Many leaders and audiences know James Baker Jr. as an agent of change.

He is an avid writer, where daily inspirations are penned to offer counsel to a plethora of followers found on his social media platforms.

His most engaged writings include, *Courage Doesn't Always Roar*, *Trust is an Honorable Virtue*, *Did You Know You're A Candidate for Burnout?* Plus, many more. He advocates for reconciliation and redemption through his writings, counsel, and leadership.

As a dynamic prophetic voice in the community, James Baker served as a mentor with Bronx Connect, a faith-based organization that spiritually serves the needs of youthful offenders, and a chaplain with The United Chaplains State of New York.

James is a former spiritual leader of a corporate Bible study for a Fortune 500 Company, where he served a diverse group of employees who attended weekly. He also formerly lectured at the Proverbial New York Theological Seminary as an Adjunct Professor.

He holds a B.S. in Labor Relations & Human Resources, a Master of Divinity, and a Masters of Religious Education from New York Theological Seminary. James is a devoted husband to Mrs. Robin Baker and a loving father and grandfather. Consultant Certifications: Diversity & Inclusion; Church Consultation University and Johnny Wimbrey Speaker's Mastery Class.